W9-CCN-232

To Professor Brent Porter
for his help in researching this project
both in his classroom at Pratt Institute, Brooklyn,
and on-site in Peru.

LOST CITY
The Discovery of
Machu Picchu

Patricia Lee Gauch, editor

Book design by Semadar Megged.
The text is set in 14.75-point Legacy Bold.
The illustrations are rendered in watercolor.

Library of Congress Cataloging-in-Publication Data
Lewin, Ted. Lost city : the discovery of Machu Picchu / Ted Lewin.
p. cm.
Summary: In 1911, Yale professor Hiram Bingham discovers a lost
Incan city with the help of a young Peruvian boy.
1. Machu Picchu Site (Peru)—Juvenile literature. 2. Yale Peruvian
Expedition, 1911—Juvenile literature. [1. Machu Picchu Site (Peru)
2. Yale Peruvian Expedition, 1911.] I. Title.
F3429.1.M3 L49 2003
985'.37—dc21
2002004461

ISBN 0-399-23302-4
10 9 8 7 6 5 4 3 2 1
First Impression

LOST
CITY

The Discovery of
Machu Picchu

Ted Lewin

Philomel Books • New York

In his first journey to South America, Yale professor Hiram Bingham longed to explore the hidden lands that lay beyond the snowcapped peaks of the Andes. Legend had it that the lost city of the Inca, Vilcapampa, lay there. Bingham was determined to discover it. So in 1910 the Yale Peruvian Expedition was organized. Finally, in July 1911, Bingham and his fellow adventurers arrived in Cusco, the first capital city of the Inca. What lay ahead for them was far from what they had expected. And more amazing. Our story begins high in the mountains of Peru. . . .

The boy looked out at the cloud-covered peaks all around him. Already his papa was working in the terraced fields. But last night he had dreamed of a tall stranger carrying a small black box. He could not get the dream out of his mind.

Suddenly, the clouds burned off and the mountains were bathed in glorious light. The dream foretold of something wonderful, he was sure.

Sixty miles south, in Cusco, Hiram Bingham gazed thoughtfully at the old Incan stone wall. He had come to Peru in search of Vilcapampa, the lost city of the Inca. But right here was the most beautiful stonework he had ever seen—huge stones cut so perfectly that not even a razor blade could be slipped between them.

The Inca had no iron tools to carve them, no wheel or draft animals to move them. The wall had withstood time and earthquakes. How had the Inca built them!

It was a mystery.

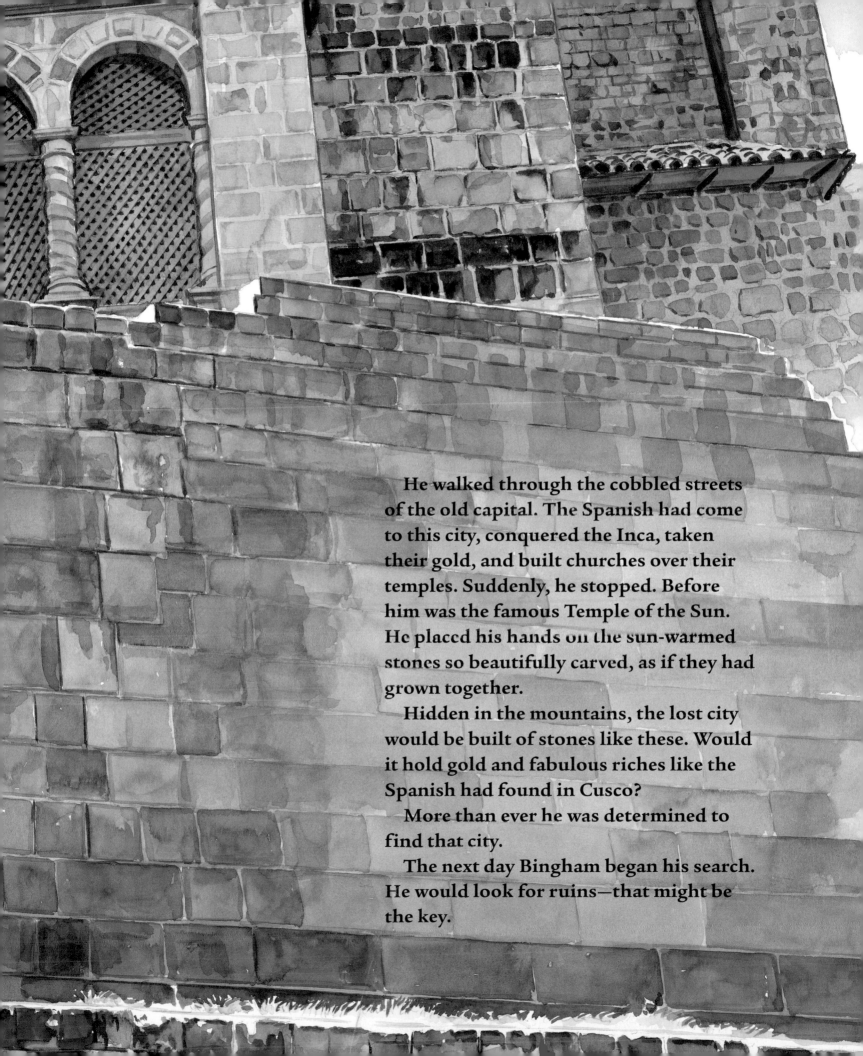

He walked through the cobbled streets of the old capital. The Spanish had come to this city, conquered the Inca, taken their gold, and built churches over their temples. Suddenly, he stopped. Before him was the famous Temple of the Sun. He placed his hands on the sun-warmed stones so beautifully carved, as if they had grown together.

Hidden in the mountains, the lost city would be built of stones like these. Would it hold gold and fabulous riches like the Spanish had found in Cusco?

More than ever he was determined to find that city.

The next day Bingham began his search. He would look for ruins—that might be the key.

He and his party, accompanied by military escort Sergeant Carrasco, left by mule train for the sacred valley of the Urubamba River.

They came to the sleepy old village of Ollantaytambo, long ago an important city. Its ancient stone terraces stepped up into the clouds.

"Are there any ruins nearby?" Bingham asked. He went door to door. He sat for hours in the cantina. "Are there any ruins near here?" he asked anyone who came in. "Do you know of the lost city of Vilcapampa?" No one knew of it.

Traveling north, the adventurers came upon a remote and wild canyon. Granite cliffs rose thousands of feet above the roaring rapids of the Urubamba River. In the distance were snowcapped mountains over three miles high. Bingham's determination to find the lost city grew with each turn of the increasingly wild trail.

Meanwhile, high on one of these granite ridges, the boy tried to help his papa on the terraces. But he couldn't shake the dream from his mind. Who was this stranger with the black box? When would he come? What was in the black box? Anxiously, he searched the mountains for a sign.

Far below in the valley, Bingham's party camped on a sandy beach alongside the thundering rapids of the Urubamba. Days had gone by. He was tired and discouraged. No one knew of any ruins.

But now the travelers aroused the curiosity of a local farmer named Arteaga.

"Are there ruins nearby?" Bingham asked when Arteaga ventured into camp.

This time, through the interpreter, the farmer said, "Yes. There are very good ruins on top of the mountain called Machu Picchu."

The farmer pointed straight up.

"Can you take us there?" Bingham asked.

"No," said Arteaga. "It is a very hard climb and there are many snakes." Bingham offered him coins. Arteaga nodded—he would show them the way.

Arteaga led them down the river trail. Suddenly, he plunged into the jungle. Bingham and the sergeant followed Arteaga through dense undergrowth down to the very edge of the river to a flimsy bridge made of slim logs. What was he getting himself into!

Sergeant Carrasco and Arteaga took off their shoes and crossed easily, gripping with their bare feet. Bingham was terrified—he crept across the bridge on hands and knees. One slip and he would be dashed to pieces in the roaring torrent below.

They climbed the bank into dense
jungle. Now the slopes were slippery
and the heat terrible. Arteaga had
warned them of the fer-de-lance, a
very venomous snake. Bingham's
eyes searched the jungle.

Up and up they climbed. The wide
river was now but a silver thread, far
below. Arteaga could think of nothing
but the fer-de-lance; Sergeant Carrasco
thought about his good, sturdy shoes;
Bingham thought of nothing but the
lost city. They cut their way through
tangled thickets. Up and up they
climbed.

Had an hour passed? Two? Three?
Now they crept on all fours. They
slipped and slid. In some places, they
held on by their fingertips.

Finally, thirsty and exhausted, they broke through the jungle into sunlight. Above them stood a little Quechua boy beside a stone hut. What could he be doing at the top of this mountain?

"*Ama llulla, ama quella, ama su'a*" (Don't lie, don't be lazy, don't steal), the boy called out in the traditional Quechua greeting.

It was the tall stranger from his dream. Carrying the black box!

The boy's whole family crowded around to greet the exhausted travelers, then brought gourds of cool water and boiled sweet potatoes.

Bingham, still gasping for breath, asked, "Where are the ruins?"
The boy said, *"Amuy, amuy!"* (Come, come!)

Bingham and the sergeant left Arteaga behind and followed at the boy's urging. *"Amuy, amuy!"* he kept saying.

At first they saw only stone terraces like the ones they had seen at Ollantaytambo. They looked as if they had been recently cleared of jungle and the vegetation burned off in order to plant crops.

But there were no ruins. Just more jungle beyond. Bingham had climbed this mountain and found—no lost city.

"Amuy, amuy!" Still, the boy beckoned him into the jungle beyond. Weary and discouraged, Bingham followed. At first all he saw were bamboo thickets and more tangled vines. Then he looked closer. Through the vines, he saw—stones. Inca stones. Then walls, beautiful stone walls! They were covered with mosses. And trees.

"Jaway, jaway!" (See, see!) the boy whispered, pointing ahead to a curved stone wall. Bingham pushed his way to it and placed his hands on the fine granite stones. A sun temple. More beautiful even than the one in Cusco.

They came to a grand stone staircase.
Where could this lead? What else was here?
"*Jaway, jaway,*" the boy called.

At the top of the staircase was a clearing. A small vegetable garden, and then . . . a temple built of enormous stones. Grander than any Bingham had ever seen. It stole his breath away.

Something was going on here, he could sense it. Something just beyond his eyes. What was it?

He followed the boy to another temple. As magnificent. This one had three windows. But now he looked across the countryside. He looked past the thickets, past the vines. He began to see the outlines of stone streets and stone cottages. He began to see the outlines of a city!

"Here, boy," he said as he opened the black box that he had been carrying, extended the bellows and focused his camera.

The first picture would be of the boy. The boy who had led him to Vilcapampa, lost city of the Incas.

But about this Bingham was wrong. When the vines were removed and the tales told, he had discovered not Vilcapampa, but a place even more amazing.

He had stumbled on Machu Picchu, a city lost in time, a city lost in the clouds.

AUTHOR'S NOTE

To research this book on the discovery of Machu Picchu, I first read Hiram Bingham's journal. In it he tells how a little Quechua boy led him to the site in the jungle. Then I traveled to Peru and followed in Hiram's footsteps as closely as I could.

I traveled to Ollantaytambo, as Hiram did, climbed the ancient terraces there, and sat in a little cantina, maybe the very one in which Hiram sat. I walked part of the rugged Inca trail to Pisac, and finally arrived at the Sun Gate above Machu Picchu.

I also journeyed through the sacred valley of the Urubamba River to Machu Picchu, and spent a week exploring and photographing the site and its surrounding cloud forest. And from the high pastures, I witnessed the magical sunset that I tried to capture on the jacket painting.

But the day the story began to come alive in my mind was the day I saw a young Quechua boy who raced our bus 2,500 feet down the mountain from Machu Picchu to the valley below—and won. As he stood, dripping with perspiration and chest heaving with exertion, I thought that Hiram's young guide must have looked just like this boy.

The most exciting part of working on the paintings was re-creating the way Machu Picchu must have looked when Hiram Bingham discovered it, hidden by five hundred years of jungle growth.

—Ted Lewin

ABOUT THE EXCAVATION OF MACHU PICCHU

After Hiram's discovery, he and his fellow archaeologists could hardly wait to explore the ruins of the lost city. Would they find skeletons? Treasure? Valuable information about the way the ancient Inca had lived and built their remarkable cities? Before they could find out, they needed to clear away the dense jungle growth that covered the site. So the next year, in 1912, the National Geographic Society and Yale University sponsored a follow-up expedition to Machu Picchu.

Their first order of business was to build a bridge across the Urubamba River at the place Hiram had crossed the previous year by crawling across logs. It took two days of difficult work and ingenuity felling trees and maneuvering them into place. At last they were ready to set up camp, but they had to make the precarious climb and get food for the workers. For three days, they hacked a trail up the mountain so their Indian bearers could bring the sixty-pound boxes of food up to camp. This trail would also serve to bring the ninety-pound boxes of specimens and pot shards down to the mule trail by the river.

Once they were at the top, the work could begin. Crews of Indians began clearing away the jungle on the site and drying and burning the debris. They didn't know what they would find beneath the tangle of jungle, but they hoped for specimens that would give them clues about who lived here and how they lived. Of course, they hoped for treasure. However, after one week of hard labor, they had found no bones, no bronze implements or pots, no gold. All the while they worked, they were plagued by venomous snakes that could bring death with every stone the workers overturned.

Finally, they found an ancient graveyard and excavated fifty-two ancient graves. Here is where they found unexpected treasure. Not gold, but skeletons, pots, tools, and bronze ornaments. One was a pin decorated with the head of a hummingbird, another a knife with the head of a llama. In all, fifty cases of shards, two hundred little bronzes, and many pots were found.

Four hard months later, the site was cleared. Gigantic trees were removed without damaging the beautiful stone walls. Terraces cleared of cane in September had to be re-cleared in November. In just two months, the cane had grown to five feet.

Once the site was revealed, Hiram could see how the ancient city had been built using nature itself to protect it. On the south side, he could see the outer stone wall, a dry moat, then an inner, twenty-foot-high wall of huge boulders for defense. On the north side, a sheer precipice. The city was impenetrable. He saw many narrow streets and rock-hewn staircases; houses one and a half stories high with gabled ends; fountains and baths to fill water pots; gateways between neighborhoods—all with different stonework—and, of course, the magnificent temples.

Again, he marveled at what master builders the early inhabitants were. He still did not know—nor has anyone firmly claimed to know—who these Inca were, nor why they deserted the village. But he had come to know how they lived, worshipped, and created one of the most remarkable cities of all time.

SOURCES

Bingham, Hiram. "In the Wonderland of Peru." *National Geographic*, vol. XXIV, no. 4 (April 1913): 387–573.

——. *Lost City of the Incas: The Story of Machu Picchu and Its Builders.* New York: Atheneum, 1969.

PRONUNCIATION GUIDE TO SPANISH AND QUECHUA WORDS
(in order of their appearance in the book)

SPANISH WORDS:

Machu Picchu: MAH-choo PEE-choo
Vilcapampa: VIL-kah-PAHM-pah
Cusco: KOOS-koh
Urubamba: oo-roo-BAHM-bah
Ollantaytambo: oh-YAWN-tay-TOM-boh
Arteaga: ar-tay-AH-gah

QUECHUA WORDS:

Quechua: KECH-wah
Ama llulla, ama quella, ama su'a: AH-mah
    LOO-lee-ah, AH-mah KWAY-yah,
    AH-mah SOO-ah
Amuy: AH-mooey
Jaway: HA-way